AF580613

A Solitary Witch Brews Self-Love

Crystal Jackson

Featuring Art by Christina Nicole

A Solitary Witch Brews Self-Love

A Book of Poetry and Prose

By Crystal Jackson

All rights reserved. No part of this publication may be reproduced, distributed, or transmitted in any form by any means, including photocopying, recording, or other electronic methods without the prior written permission of the author, except in the case of brief quotations embodied in reviews and certain other noncommercial uses permitted by copyright law. For permission requests, write to the author's email address below.

Please do not participate in or encourage piracy of copyrighted materials in violation of the author's rights. Purchase only authorized material.

Cover Art: Christina Nicole

Copyright © 2022 Crystal Jackson

All rights reserved.

ISBN

Crystal Jackson
www.crystaljacksonwriter.com
crystaljackson.writer@outlook.com
www.medium.com/@CrystalJackson
FB & IG @CrystalJackson.writer
Twitter @cjacksonwriter

Christina Nicole
www.instagram.com/christinanicole.art

To Stephanie

&

To the magic women of YTT 2022

Renee, Sue, Natalia, Susan, Jamie, Kate, Shelagh, & Barb

The circle is open – but never broken.

Contents

You are magic.

Come and read a spell.

Tea-Stained Pages

Water hot and clouds of steam
I try to catch my breath
I stand beneath the water hot
Until no heat is left

Wrap bath sheet thick and warm around
Smooth lotion in a honey scent
Pull on pajamas laundered fresh
The morning light's a soft blush hint

Clouds of steam follow me
Down light steps as quiet as a dream
The water rush and kettle on
Til water hot and clouds of steam

Interrupt my reading with a whisper
Interrupt again with a sharp scream
Quick steps answer, kettle calms
Tea leaves brew and hint at dreams

While I rustle-turn another page
Swirled honeyed sweetness in my tea
Obscuring tea leaf messages
That might have meant so much to me

Hot, blow, sip and sip again
The pages turn and daylight climbs
Across flowers, walls, lights on my book
Luxuriating, stretching time.

Independent Lament

I am so self-sufficient that it hurts
My back breaks and aches
Beneath the weight
Of all the things I can do alone
Like pay the bills
And sort the kids
And cry alone
And hold myself still
Beneath the grief
The weight of age
The written word
And turning page
Watch the way I can do it all
Alone.

In Remembrance of a Muse

Early morning waking slow
Intertwined so thoroughly
With arms and legs and beating hearts
I did not want to let you go

Your kind eyes, your stretching smile
Drew me in and made me dream
Or was it the way you were listening
That made me want to stay a while

Unwilling muse, my ghostly vision
You would leave and break my heart
I'd have let you go to love another
But the silence wasn't my decision

Still, it should comfort you to know
That other loves have come since then
And left my heart broken further
Years after I have let you go

You were my first muse and my last
I am my own inspiration
I draw my power from myself now
And make you a footnote in my past

Early morning waking slow
I remember being intertwined
When I could not separate yours or mine
Before you left and I let go

But, once, we woke up intertwined
Once, you reached in the night for me
Once, your smile was for me alone
But I lost me when you were mine

I let the memory dissolve once more
Muses aren't welcome here anymore.

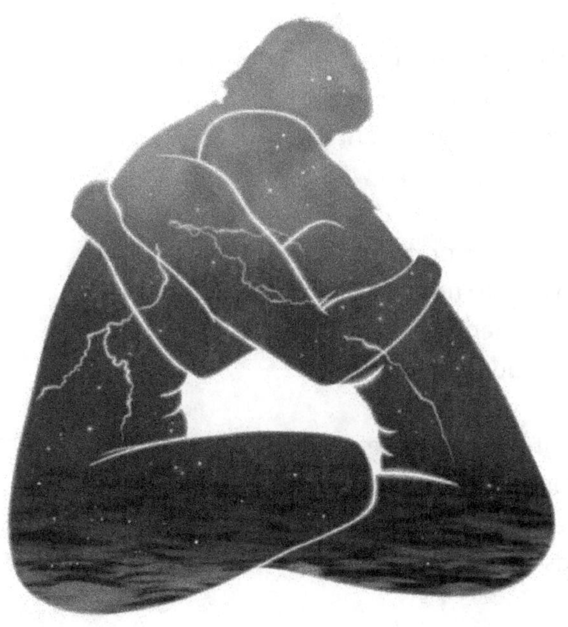

A Solitary Witch Brews Self-Love

I made this brew on my own
I crafted it when I was alone
It was enough, I had all I could need.
But a longing grew, became a seed

Then, I met you on a changing wind
You overflowed my cup and then
You began to think I needed you,
To mix up a strong enough love to brew.

The winds changed again, as they often will,
You started to guess how I might feel,
You began to fear that I might fall
But read the runes, what's writ on the wall.

Read the tea leaves or my hand
If you ever want to understand,
The lines in my hand will tell it true
I wanted but had no need of you.

I make this brew, I read the cards
I cast the spells, I watch the stars
I give my heart free reign to roam
Until it lands and finds a home,

But it can take flight once again
If home's a place it can't get in
And I'll be here, mixing my brew
That never had the need of you.

So, take care and count the hours
But never underestimate my power
Or assume it comes from what you bring
I never needed anything.

But wanted, yes, a hand to hold
A home with a hearth to warm the cold
A love that's stronger than the doubt
One that no darkness could drive out,

But I can take flight on my own
And brew the love I need alone.

Fortuitous Tea

Water swirls inside your cup
Unfurling tea leaves as you wait
You'd gulp it down instead of sip
But her head gives the slightest shake
To say fortunes are never rushed,
Or late

Bitter is the tea to taste
But honey softens its sharp bite
You take the time to slowly savor
As the day shifts into darkening night
She strikes the match
For candlelight

Only then, she'll put the cup aside
And reach to take your outstretched palm
She'll trace your lifeline with fingertips
While waiting for the leaves to calm
Her words a murmur,
Her touch a balm

She reads the tea, your cards, your hands
She'll see your life writ in those lines
The loves you find but cannot keep
The ones who'll see you
Safe through time
The life that's yours
If you heed the signs

Tea leaves dance and form a dream
She'll translate the visions that appear
And leave you full of restless wanting
For all you want but still fear
She'll smile softly
Before she'll disappear

Inside the curtain, steps grow faint
She'll return with a gift inside her hands
And hold it out for you to take
As if taking it, you'll understand
That a candle given is choice
And not demand

You'll light the candle in a darkened room
Alone at last and in your space
Surrounded by your favorite things
The light reflected on your face
Across the walls
Shadows give chase

Then remember her slow words
The way they wrapped you in their grip
You'll brew the tea she gifted you
And know your power in every sip
You'll let a smile
Hover on your lips.

I Love Her

Power returns
When he leaves
But at first, I only feel the grief
The sting of pain
Crushing rejection
The devastation of his relief
He sighs, lighter, as he goes
Even as I weep

Power grows
Unseen, unnoticed
Beneath the anguish of broken dreams
It knits itself
From love left over
It weaves the spell
And mends the seams
Of wistful longing
For loved lost things

Power waits
Then builds and shimmers
Until I step up to wear its crown
The knowledge settles
Like a promise
The strength that fuels me
Circles 'round
The hum of magic
Is comfort to me now

Power arrives
I wear it softly
But at first, I only feel its glow
The way it elevates
My truth
The way it doesn't waver
But merely knows
I honor the knowing
And my power grows

Power returns
I turn to hold her
I love her as I should have always done
When I was putting
Others first
When they all left
She did not run
I love myself
I am The One

Power stays
Even when he goes
But at first, I struggle in my pain
The scream of grief
And devastation
I make a prayer
From just his name
He is lighter as he leaves
But I am not the same

But power grows
When lovers leave

The choice they make bears a great cost
But it is not my price
To keep paying
When they leave
All is not lost
I love her now
Just as I ought

And power rests
Upon my crown
Lightly, lightly, still, it grows
I honor love
As I have felt it
And I honor when it goes
The power stays
From my pen flows

I am not the same
As I once was, and the power
Is not hidden inside my frame
I take back my prayer
And remake it
Stronger, softer
In my name.

The Star

Constellations in my palms
She smiles, contented, looking down
But the world outside is rocky still
Can luck flourish on such shaky ground?

She doesn't answer, doesn't waver
Just holds my eyes until it's clear
The future is inside my hands
What I'll do or won't is waiting here

For me to choose, for me to try
The luck will grow if I nurture its' seed
Thorns might cross my path at times
But wildflowers bloom from neglected weeds

I close my hand, take it to heart
The stars tell a story I could live
If I but open my heart, my mind
If my hands are open to help and give

The luck I'll make in the life I lead
With every moment filled with grace
Shared times and sacred solitude
The times love has shown upon my face

I smile, contented, third eye open
The constellations dance and wait
Inside my hands, the future's written
Call it luck or work, magic or fate.

Dark Magic

Magic potion in my hands
Dark magic in this brew
If I take it to my lips,
I'll be transported back to you
Another day, another spell
A trance I cannot break
I sipped a different potion then
But what difference did it make?

Flames illuminated us
We leaned closer to the fire
As if the heat could save us
From curiosity or desire

Or perhaps we weren't after saving
We simply didn't feel the burn
But when the trance was broken
It was I who had to learn

New life, new spell, a different me
A quiet incantation
I could not bring you back to me
Through magic invitation

I could not be who I once was
I transformed into a different beast
Sipping different magic potions
With intoxicating feasts

But one small sip from this dark brew
And I am rising higher
Above the ones we used to be
Illuminated by the fire

Still, I sip and am transported
To what has become my witching hour
The who I was before who I am
Finally found her greatest power

Magic potion, feel the heat
Feel the power of temptation
Then return to life again
With another sip and incantation.

A Swing and a Miss

He was easy to love
And easy to lose
I was harder to know
Even harder to choose

I lost all my senses
Love tore them apart
I was swinging for fences
With a wide-open heart

He was already gone
Before I began
I was running the bases
For dark, empty stands

He was easy to love
But then, what was I?
I was an open-heart yearning
Under a perfect blue sky.

A Vigil for the Last Lover

Light a candle for the lover
Who came before
Pour wine into my glass
And tell me more

Tell me all the ways
You tried to make her stay
I will hold it against you
When you let me get away

Play the same old song
Dance to the same old tune
When you think of dancing under stars
You don't think of me and you

Did the kisses shared
Mean nothing more than this
A substitute for the one you love
And hate and yet still miss

You play your tune
I'll be here playing mine
Love unreturned then lost
To the sound of pouring wine

I'll light a candle inside a star
A vigil to my feeling
And summon words to dispel
This holding on,
for healing.

Bait and Switch

Lovers whisper lies
That they believe
Rather earnest in their hope
Than trying to deceive

Still, we take the bait
And bite
To come up gasping
Broken
From the fight

Of loving
Even when the love's not right
Hope draining
As we drown
In air and light

Perfect Wife or Perfect Life?

I remember shaping dreams
Around your life
Turning myself into your
Perfect wife
With neither promise, hope,
Nor shiny ring
I turned myself into
Your everything

I made myself indispensable
It's true
And shaped myself around
Each "I love you"
To make myself worthy
For you to choose
All I had left was
Me to lose.

Pink Champagne

Bubbles dance inside my glass
Rising, swirling in the light
The blush-tint hue touches
Blush-stained lips
One sip only
To invoke one night
The stars above were near to touch
And the city lights spun out
Like stars below
I was caught inside a gaze
My hand in his
Lit by a candle's glow
His name in my mouth
Was an incantation
His lips tasted of pink champagne
His eyes were bright
With dark temptation
To murmur and to moan his name
Bubbles dance and rise again
Another memory comes to mind
Of peaches tasted,
Dripping, wet
In the summer sun
The sin was mine
Or bubbles tasted on a cold, wild day
The wind whipped sand into my hair
But his hand pulled
The tendrils loose
And wrapped them in his fist
To hold them there

Bubbles rise up
To dance in the light
A joy I can sip and remember
If I can hold the pain at bay
If I can forget that
Dark December
They say I'm holding onto grief
Not drawing poison
From my heart and head
I toast the night with
Pink champagne
And see a sunrise from a hotel bed
Salt tears trace down a windowpane
The night's bright stars
Both blur and waver
His name in my mouth,
An incantation
I need to spit out
Where I once savored
The name is a spell I do not cast
Yet, the ghost of us still lingers on
Summoned by the blush
Of pink champagne
No matter the time
Since he's been gone
My heart is a relic
That won't move on
My memory is a palace
With a secret door
Bubbles dance in this reliquary
When they disappear,
I pour one more.

The Mountain

(a PMDD Journey)

Every month, I build self-love
From the ground up
From the four corners of my feet
To the crown drawing up
Heart open, eyes ahead
I am stronger than I've been
Feeling blessed with every breath
I love myself again
My energy is strong
Strength glows from my eyes
Standing rooted in love
I rise

Then an avalanche of despair
Comes cascading down
Sending the self-love
That I've built
Straight down to the ground
Head down and heart wrecked
I struggle to breathe
Struggling for self-worth
For the strength
To believe

I lie down on the ground
Like the dead looking up
And let the earth hold me
As I refill my cup
I'm rooted and safe
I keep speaking the words

But the sky doesn't hear me
The silence remains
Undisturbed

Still, I just lie there
And mourn the mountain that fell
And the heights I once climbed
Before I landed
In my personal hell
I let the earth hold me
Until trembling, I stand
With a sun breath to the sky
As life shakes my heart,
Takes my hand

From falling to rising
My eyes look ahead
And the view is a reminder
I'm not better off dead
I take deep, slow breaths
Feel the roots growing down
I open my heart
Feel the strength of my crown

I build back the self-love
It's the mountain I climb
I hold onto the peace
Knowing it's only a matter of time
Until the world shakes
And I am left on my own
Rebuilding my mountain
Of self-love alone.

To Love You, Still

sometimes, i think aloud
"i still love you"
with wonder
and endeavor not to count
the days since you left

but other times, i think
"i love you, still"

as in, i love you as you were
when you walked toward me
with purpose, your eyes sparkling
brighter than the stars in the sky
when first we kissed

as in, i love you then
when the thought of getting to me
consumed you
when you would bend toward me,
lips brushing my neck
as we walked to the car,
how your body melted into mine
before the doors even closed
how you focused on me
and i focused on driving faster

as in, i love you then
when the future appeared
in the distance like a place
we'd visit together

when i carefully held up
all my broken pieces
like a mirror
and trusted you to see me
through them, to love me
through them

as in, i love you then
when your voice on the line
was an anchor in a storm
i didn't yet understand,
when i would reach for you
to find you reaching back

i love you, still
when the words fell easily
from your lips
and i tasted them like honey
when i hadn't yet been judged
as falling short
when you said i would always
be enough, when maybe
you believed i could be
and i believed it too

but i still love you

i still love you
even though the last words
exchanged between us
left remnants of smoke in the air
charred bits of dreams
still fall like ash

and the words your friend
whispered at a party
in an alcohol haze
were suddenly revealed
as prophecy

but i still love you
even though your anger
is directly proportionate
to my grief, and your doubt
that i still grieve at all
only multiplies with time
how it seems impossible
for you to believe that anyone
could love you and see you
and see you and know you
and love you all the same

now i'm left loving me
quietly in the morning when i wake
and forgive myself
for missing you still
and midday when a stray thought
turns a laugh suddenly
into a choked cry
and again in the evening
when i tell myself, sternly,
to dream a new dream
with someone else
who could love me and see me
and see me and know me
and love me all the same.

Love Between the Lines

Put me back on paper
Leave me right there on the page
Where you thought that you could love me
Before you realized your mistake

Write to me of poetry
Build a lovely, fragile dream
But live it with me on the page
Where I am exactly what I seem

Traced in ink and solid lines
That never tremble, fear, or waver
Where I am powerful and bold
A vision to be held, and savored

One-dimensional, it's true
But she'll light up your eyes
I won't see the creeping disappointment
Darken into something you despise

Or wonder why the paper version
Is the one that you would choose
It breaks my heart you'll grieve her going
But me, you'll gladly lose.

I Tried to Make a Home of You

I tried to make a home of you
To build family from the love in me
I constructed futures on my own
I built my dreams so quietly
That you probably never even knew
That I was building home
From me and you

I tried to make an anchor out of you
Something to hold me near the shore
A foundation built of sand and sea
Of love and hope and little more
And now I am set adrift
Through memories, like sand,
I sit and sift

I tried to make a story from our love
The kind we'd read, and read again
An epic love to warm our life together
Before I knew you wouldn't let me in
I got tired of knocking on that door
I don't come around
Knocking anymore

I tried to make the love I felt enough
I tried to make a lifetime of our days
I held on to every moment spent
Now I watch them dissolve into the waves

My love was ever-steady, ever-true
I sit and watch the sea return
My love to you

Time and tides, a year, another age
I will work to build a home of me
I'll write my life like words across a page
Missing you but never missing me
I will love, I will breathe again
Moving to higher ground
I will begin.

How I Knew He Wasn't Mine to Keep

This is how I knew
He wasn't mine to keep
The world was ending
And he did not come to me

Miles stretched and the silence
Of what he did not say
Crackled on the line like static
Empty storefronts faced empty streets
And still he did not come

Masked faces with anxious eyes
Passed in hurried steps
Doors shut inward, teddy bears
Hunched hopefully on windowsills
And still he did not come

Packages arrived in tidy boxes
While doors stayed tightly shut
And still he did not come
Spring blossoms withered in summer heat
Leaves fell and a cold wind blew them
In skittering circles down sidewalks
Before they were whisked away
Shuddering against closed doors
And still he did not come

When doors began opening
When faces began to turn, tentatively,
Toward new days and half-smiling faces
Still, he did not come

When help arrived with a pinprick
And a bandage, and my mask
Slid down at long last
Still, he did not come

Then the call came
And I knew
He would never come for me
Again.

Forgiving You for Me

There's grace in the space
Between my hands and these keys
Between the words in my heart
I will type but not speak
Between the hurt I have felt
And the love I've freely given
I come now to grace and not anger
To say you are forgiven

I forgive your defensiveness
Your sharp edge of anger
How you were my favorite person
Who became this bitter stranger
I forgive you for staying
When you could see my heart bleeding
I forgive you for not feeling
The love I was desperately needing

I forgive you for withdrawing
While I was still caught in my feelings
I forgive you, I forgive you
For me, for my healing
There's grace in the space
Between your heart and my own
I hope you find what you're needing
I hope you won't be alone

My words fall on the page
Their black and white bleeding
This forgiveness and grace
You won't be reading, or needing

But the words as they fall
Finally set my heart free
I forgive you, I forgive you

Even if you never forgive me.

A Ghost Story

The steady scratch across the floor
A branch against the window frame
That is all I hear right now
As I sweep aside my pain

I banish dust and turn on the lights
I cannot remain unchanged
I shake the yellow rug outside
But I don't speak your name

I sprinkle salt in thick white lines
And smoke out the past we knew
I can't make new bones of this old house
But it can see the last of you

I clean the windows 'til they shine
I mop and wax the floor
I make each swipe a prayer for peace
A wish to be free of you once more

I change the locks and hide the key
I take the deepest breath
I am free to live in love
Now that the ghosts have finally left.

She Calls Her Power Back

Her hands on you, a sweet delight
Her eyes found yours throughout the night
Her heart was melted wax inside your hands
You turned an hourglass and watched the sands

She gave her time - you watched hers drain out
She pledged her faith - you plunged her in doubt
But rising through the dark, she grew
Into a woman of strength with no need of you

She strikes the notes and plays the chords
She reads the cards and draws the Swords
She calls her power and chooses her time
What once was yours is now only mine

A candle burns bright, a wax-melting glory
She spins the tale and writes her story
She wears the crown, a flower-wreathed altar
Her steps against the Earth won't stop or falter

She'll leave you to wonder
When she already knows
You'll follow the breadcrumbs
But they won't reach where she goes.

Serving Size

Salt circle and candle flame
I drink my wine
But taste your name

I call to my power
To drive you out
The curse of loving
And being left with doubt

I come quiet now
To reclaim what's mine
No scrying mirror
No divining signs

Just self-love served up
With wine.

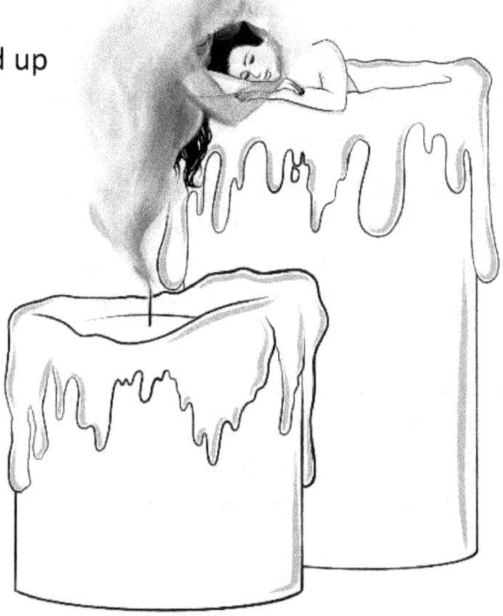

Framed

Did you find yourself drawn in
Penciled in with scrawls
Shaded with your secret sin
A box, once drawn,
Could not be escaped again

Did you try to break free of her lines
By adding distance first
Then adding up her crimes
As if pointing out her flaws
Would make not loving her align

Did she trap you neatly there in ink
Trace your features first with love
Then blot them out with drink
Burn them then in effigy
Hurt taken to the brink

Did you find yourself skewered on her pen
Caught up in words you never heard
Because she could not let you in
Not when she saw you pack your things
Not when she was being left again

She'll write the words, and won't you find your own?
The way you'll tell the world she's wrong
The way she'll walk the world alone
Her steps on this Earth a warning song
Her voice to the sky an unsettling tone

Nothing is as clear, no warning bell
As a sharpened pen
Dipped in a blood-drawn well
The price of love
And a healing spell

Framed up with love and a broken heart
She heals herself with words
But splinters the world you knew apart
She might have warned you, a little,
At the start.

The Horror Show

Thumbs move quick
To strike the keys
And shadows grow
From twisted trees
The wind, it shrieks
The leaves rush by
Waiting for runes
To form replies
The air grows cool
The clouds rush past
The moon's grim grin
Reveals itself at last
Runes disappear
And horror sets in
The moment you know
You've been ghosted

Again.

The Only Witness

Bare feet on sidewalk
Silent steps
The moon above with slyest smile
Watches the path diverge
With a knowing air
And decides to stay to watch awhile

Bare feet step slowly
Through the cool, soft grass
A whisper caress against bare skin
A flower blooms
Scent but not seen
Leaves fall down
In joyous dash, dance, spin

Bare feet strike earth
Then arms boldly rise
Toward jewel-strewn midnight sky
Chanting soft words
You'll strain to hear
Without understanding why

Bare feet reverse
The silent steps
The night's a cloak
Held close and dear
A smile on lips lights up the dark
With only the moon to witness
What happened here

Bare feet on sidewalk
Silent steps
A door opens softly, closes again
Night blooms unfurl
Scent but not seen
Leaves land lightly from one last spin

The soft wind whispers
Through quiet trees
No one around to strain to hear
The world turns softly
In restless dreams
The moon the only witness here.

In Sunlight and Shadows

Sunlight and shadows
Your hand in mine
Your pulse against my skin
Your lips slowing time

Wine glasses on a table
Neglected at last
Joined by items of clothing
Your past and my past

Hours to linger
To taste, touch, and savor
No room for doubts here
No thought yet to waver

Only kisses and whispers
And begging for more
Against walls and steamed windows
From the bed to the floor

From sunlight to shadows
A break, then a pause
Before we come back together
Joined by love and a cause

A sigh and a murmur
As the last chapter is read
Then, I drain the wine glasses
And go up, alone, to my bed.

Ghosts in the House at Nightfall

Every joy has a twin,
A sharp edge of pain
I'm cut up and bleeding
Just the same
No memory is safe
From being destroyed
Lovers keep leaving
Even friends leave their void
And I am left shaken
By all that I'm losing
Left cut up, and fucked up
With scars and bright bruising
Every memory I'd keep
Becomes grist for the mill
Of words I keep writing
Because there's too much
Space left to fill
The absence takes space
Sucks the air from my lungs
Yet, I just keep climbing
Though I hang from these rungs
The memories have sprung
Not to thrill and delight
But to haunt and remind me
That I'm lonely tonight
Every joy has a twin
A sad-smiling sorrow
I'm cut up, and fucked up
Maybe I'll heal
Tomorrow.

Downfall

I would stand, body trembling
tears streaming, words stifled
from where you hushed me
you said my anger was my problem
you said my rage would be my downfall

I grew older, taller
you tell me I shouldn't burn the bridges
you say I should try to keep the peace

everyone says my anger will be my downfall

I stand here, body trembling
words pouring as quickly as my tears
and think

everyone told me rage would be my downfall
nobody told me
it would be

love.

What If I Told the Truth?

What if I told you I couldn't write the words
Couldn't make them flow from my mind
To the end of my fingers
Hesitating above the keys
Trembling with exhaustion
Or pain
Or need
Would you read my old words again?
Would you still follow me?
If I couldn't give you another piece of myself
If I didn't have another piece to spare
If I couldn't bleed anymore on the page
Because I was too busy bleeding
Everywhere
Would you find other words to read?
Would you forget about me?
What if I didn't have another tear to shed
Or another demon to chase onto the pages
From the darkness of my head
Because it was too busy torturing me instead
And I was too busy trying to survive
To hold onto tiny moments to stay alive
What if I told you I couldn't write today
Couldn't make the words fall on the page
Too caught up in my sadness
Too tired even for rage
I couldn't make the words do what I was needing
Couldn't form the ink from all this bleeding
Too busy tying knots to pull me up
With shaking hands
I'm filling up my cup.

Better a Comma Than Stones

I curl my body into a comma
Better than a pocket full of stones
I lay still as death and as quiet
I'm lying here
Alone
Pulling air into my body
And then letting it go
Curled to protect my heart space
From a hurt you cannot know

I curl my body tighter
I try to numb the pain
I could be lying on the pavement
On a street or in the rain
And all I'd hear is breathing
Pull air in and push
It out
To the sound of my
Heart beating
As if it could get out

Drum circle of just one now
My body curled in fear
A thumping and a drumming
Between gasps and falling
Tears

I am a comma waiting
Holding space for all I feel
Not trying to deny it
Not pretending
It's not real

Better curled into a comma
Than a pocket full of stones
I'm hurting but I'm holding on
And I am not alone

Outside the drumming circle
In the world outside my tears
There is laughter waiting
And there's comfort
For my fears

But I curl into a comma
And wait until I'm able
To stand upright
And walk outside
And join you at the table.

Blame My Third Eye for the End

No palm read, no fortune told
I did not read the tea
No tarot cards, no incantation
Could spell it clear for me

No thick white lines of salt intent
No sage smoked alibi
I did not dream up all these things
I couldn't if I tried

I did not seek a guru's guide
Or wish this into being
I did not call upon my third eye
To make this clear for seeing

No illusion did I seek
No darkness did I call
I did not want to know this thing
I did not wish for this at all

Now you leave behind a path of curses
Recast my name as Bitch
But what is broken would always break
It didn't need a witch

And no foretelling was required
To determine what would be
You wanted to make me something yours
I wanted to stay me

And you will curse me for a time
You'll wish we'd never spoken
But this end was always written
And I will not be broken

And you are not a broken thing
Tossed carelessly to the floor
I’d not trade that time with you
And I’d not ask for more

But instead would bless the time we had
Thankful for all I learned
Even though I hear you curse my name
And pray for witches burned.

Mermaid Tricks

That mermaid trick
You lured me in
You tasted of salt and sweetest sin
You pulled me under, pulled me down
I could not breathe and could not drown

As far above was my whole world
But here in the dark, I was your girl
I saw your eyes, how they held my own
If I drown with you, I'm not alone

But I looked above to that glint of light
I remembered air, remembered sight
Remembered me before there was a you
And met your eyes in all that blue

Remembered sunken ships and sailors lost
The liquid graves and counted costs
And prying my hand from your own
Was a pain as sharp as I've ever known

That mermaid trick
You lured me in
You tasted of salt
I dreamed of sin

I'd have drowned with you, drowned in my tears
And loved you all my remaining years
But I'd have lost myself, drowned in the night
If I had not looked up to see the light.

Pour a Glass and Wait

I buy his favorite wine
And wait
I drink the white wine that I like best
Put cheese and crackers on a plate
His chair is empty
I watch the door
The threshold he will cross
No more

His favorite soda is kept
In my house
Snug between the juice and the milk
The only drink here
That never runs out
But sits waiting
Like I do
I don't have the heart to say
He's never coming back
For you.

I Become the Problem He Can Name

His need for validation
Fills the space between us
So I don't tell him about the creeping
Shadows hanging over me
I stroke his ego with one hand
And use the other to tuck
My depression into my back pocket
To wait for a better time

The vast wasteland of silence
In my head is a place on a map
He's never visited
Yet, he doubts it exists
Even when I drag out my luggage
And unpack it in the center
Of our relationship
Where we both trip over it

On sunshine days when his smile
Is even bigger than his presence
I don't mention my shadows
I don't want to stand there accused
Of turning a good day bad
But turning a bad day worse
Is also an unspeakable crime
So when do I get to speak
Or breathe or be?

I watch him taking up all the space
And love him for his bright light
And also his bitter shadows
But he does not see me
And what he cannot see
He can only resent, and so
I become the problem he can name
His need to get away from me grows
Until its shadow nearly surpasses my own

But outside of his shadow
And need for constant validation
I stand in the sun as I am
Shadows hug the corners of my life
But I no longer feel a need to hide them
They are and I am and it's okay
Even on days when it's not okay at all
I still love him but safely
And from a distance
Where his shadow self can no longer
Overshadow me while pointing the finger

His need for validation
Is a plea for love, but he doesn't want mine
Instead, he chases busy days
And runs from his thoughts
The way I once ran from my shadows
As if we can ever truly escape them
I hold compassion but safely
And from a distance
I practice self-compassion
Where I once practiced silence

I honor still the space between us
He fills it with anger and contempt
But I reassemble my memories without his input
I tape and glue the pieces
The way I so often have done with my heart
Handled carelessly in his hands
His impact brutal
Even with gentle intentions

My shadows are growing now
And I do not have to hide them
I tremble from the fear I cannot outrun
And wish he could have held me
Through the days I barely survived
But I hold myself instead
And count it as Enough
I count myself as Enough
I hold on through the darkness
And know that it will pass.

One Last Kiss

The last kiss didn't feel like
Goodbye
It felt like something
Sacred instead
Like a prayer from parted lips
Or holy hands
And tasting sips
Love rising up
And filling up my head

The last kiss didn't feel like
Regret
It felt like something we could do
All the days
That we'll have left
It felt like warm sun
And candle flames
Like love gift-wrapped
Around your name

The last kiss didn't feel like
The end
When you would walk back
What you said
And ask if we could
Still be friends

It didn't feel like
A friendly kiss
A parting gift, a last goodbye
It felt instead
Like something you would miss

The last kiss didn't feel like
The last

But you move on and I stand
With the others in your past
A face to blur
As time goes by
You'll forget the taste of me
And my eyes

The last kiss didn't feel like
We were through
But I'll move on knowing
Someone else
Will be kissing you

And they won't know the end
Is drawing near
They won't know you'll draw
Them close
Then leave them standing here

I'll make room
I'll move down the line
And try to tell them
Life after you
Is something close to
Fine

I'll be just another name
You once knew
You met and loved and left
When you were through.

Insomnia

Tick, tock, the clock at night
Counting hours down
The fan is spinning, spinning
I watch it go around

The stars are stretching, aching
The courthouse tolls the hour
And I am reaching, stretching
Inside me for my power

I call it to me softly
I feel it drawing near
It feeds upon my happiness
It burns away my fear

It settles down upon me
It feels like breathing deep
It wraps itself around me
And now,
At last,
I sleep.

Perilous Mood, Deepening Darkness (PMDD)

There's no perfection
Only progress
I say those words once more
Then watch the ceiling spin around
As I'm lying on the floor
I tell myself to stand up
As if it's something simple I can do
But I'm lying here
Half dying here
And there are things I wish you knew

Fourteen
Days of brain fog
I cried
Thirteen
Times today
A dozen
Times I wanted to die
Eleven
Times I chose to stay
Ten
Minutes staring at my reflection
A stranger to my eyes
Nine
Times I had to combat the thought
That I should say goodbye
Eight-
Thirty and I want to go to bed
To sleep until it's done
To count from
Seven
Days of hell

Until I see myself through to
One

I survive the cycle
Don’t say it makes me strong
I am happy half my life
The other half feels wrong
Like I’m poorly put together
And walking through the mist
Trying to remind myself
That I’m still here, I still exist
Even though the darkness
Is a siren with arms stretched wide to hold me
I remember fourteen days from now
I will become, again, the old me

The ceiling doesn’t stop its spinning
But I slowly come off the floor
Floating down the darkened hallway,
I wash up against my bedroom door
Then heave myself upon my bed
Fold blankets tight around
And, waiting for the medicine to work,
I pray I do not drown.

Haunted House

I stood there where you left me
Eaves weighted by debris
Shutters listed to the side
Water dripped into the hall
With ghost shapes of furniture,
Sheet-draped and desolate,
Marked by dust motes in light
Filtered in through cracked windows
The screen door struck the house
As the wind whispered
You were never coming back
Dust swirled down the hall
As the curtains reached, reached for you
But one day, I woke up and saw
A clear space in a corner of the window
Outside, wildflowers grew through sidewalk cracks
Covering the steps you took away from me
So, I cleaned the window
And went back to bed
I woke up to sunlight and the sight
Of a field cut through by a lovely stream
So, I swept all the floors
And dusted the shelves
Then, I ate an apple I found
Discarded on the table
Like you discarded me
And then went back to sleep
The next day, I pulled sheets off furniture
And listened to them tell your memory
To hush before billowing in the light
And falling softly to the floor
I gathered them in my arms
And washed them by hand in the lovely stream
Then carried them, dripping,
To dance on the line in the sunlight

When cars drive by, they don't hurry along
They slow down and wonder what it is
About this old house that positively gleams
Despite age and hardship
And how it stands all alone in the field
The jut of its eaves defiant

I was a boarded-up house when we were through
But I didn't stay that way

Did you?

The Sun Rises, And So Do I

The morning kiss of cool air on skin
The warmth of the sun rising slowly into view
I'm drinking coffee and breathing in
But there was a time I would have wished for you
When morning thoughts meant you and me
And futures built themselves from dreaming
When I loved you effortlessly
Before I finally understood your meaning

Mornings were once a dark sad thing
Where I wished I could just go on sleeping
When my heart broke on another dream
I realized could not be mine for the keeping
Tired nights faded to weary waking
The brightness served to highlight my sorrow
Life was waiting, there for the taking
But I kept promising tomorrow

Now, I revel in mornings crisp and cool
Where the day awaits my wish and whim
I won't play love's lonely fool
I won't put life on hold to dream of him
But will build dreams of my own making
I'll feel joy in my breath and bones
Love will be mine for the taking
Because I'll weave it into my life and home

The sun is rising, and I am, too
To walk the world with grit and grace
My thoughts might briefly land on you
I wonder if you feel the warmth upon your face

Or feel a chill and softly wonder why
As you turn in sleep or greet the day
The sun is higher in the sky
As I go to put this mug away

Inside, a puppy gives chase to children's laughter
I feel love in each breath and in my bones
This is my happiest ever after
There is joy in this heart and home

More joy than I have ever known.

Changing the World for Our Girls

Our girls will walk the earth
With heads held high
Their steps will be so light
They won't even notice
The dust of the patriarchy
Crumbling beneath their boots
They'll dust it off and keep walking

Because our girls have places to go
They're riding rockets toward a sky
With no glass ceiling, only endless blue stretches
And soft white clouds made for dreaming.

And our girls?
They dream

Their dreams are not nightmare screams
Of unwanted hands,
Fists clutching sheets, waking
Sweat-drenched and fear-cloaked.

Our girls sleep with smiles on their faces,
With relaxed brows and unclenched hands
That sometimes move as if they hear music.

Our girls deserve better
Than another breaking news story.
Our girls should not have to join in
And cry out Me, Too.

Our girls deserve a seat at the table
Voices equal to any man's
And the steadfast conviction
That they are, in fact, as human,
As capable, as strong as anyone else.

Our girls will be a sight to behold
Look at them walk along
No catcalls follow
No unwelcome hands reach out to touch

They will be queens
Because we said
Enough
And never again.

Look at them walking,
Eyes straight ahead
As if they never had to worry
About shadows.

Love Willfully Deceives

A woman in love sees life a different way
Ever-ready to take pleasure in what she sees
I walk these quiet streets as much in love today
With the home I once chose — or perhaps once chose me

Aging brick reaches toward the blue
The courthouse bells gently extol the time
I watch clouds and crowds aimlessly pass through
Footsteps strike sidewalks rhythmic with the chimes

Reaching up, I touch the brightest leaves
I stop to appreciate each bloom and smile
But love is a condition which often deceives
When we linger in beauty and practice kind denial

We see the beauty in cobwebs and broken parts
We note it down as yet another lovely charm
So, we don't see decay or broken hearts
We look away from all that might alarm

In my ardent admiration of my town
I failed to see a truth I can't deny
Dark faces populate the green when it's a Motown sound
White faces clutch flags on picnics each July

And little do the crowds mix on a day
The lines are drawn and I, new, cannot see
Where they are to wipe them all away
Or how to wipe those lines right out of me

Because there's beauty in this town I chose
I can't dismiss the loveliness around
But beauty is cracked sidewalks where a flower grows
And there's beauty when the line is taken down

I walk in love and try to open up my eyes
I try to see my town through another lens
I don't tell myself the kindest of the lies
I say instead this is where the work begins

To make the town's heart as lovely as its lines
The aging brick that reaches toward the blue
Taking down the segregation signs
Our hearts beating together, creating something new

I walk these quiet streets and I believe
In the town that I once chose — or once chose me
When we're in love we willfully deceive
But loving truly means we need to truly see.

Between Bootstraps & Bicycles

Every now and then,
Sadness would well up in her,
Rising like a tide
Because she was a bicycle-built-for-two kind of girl.
An initials-carved-into-a-tree girl.
A girl meant for candlelit dinners.
She dreamed in picnics and sunsets
And flowers picked by hand,
But life kept handing her
Bouquets of disappointment,
Gilded boxes of heartache,
And a permanent reservation for one.
She'd look over her children's heads
at her own reflection and say,
Aren't they grand?
We didn't do too badly after all.
And most of the time,
It was all that she needed.
But sometimes, just sometimes...
She wished for something other.
Lucky for her,
She was also a made-up-of-grit kind of girl.
A pull-herself-up-by-the-bootstraps girl.
A my-life-my-way kind of girl
She dreamed of travel
And built castles from her deepest desires,
But life kept handing her
A sense of humor, however dark,
And more strength
Than she sometimes knows what to do with.

How I Have Loved You,
How I Always Will

When my now smooth skin
Is crinkled like tissue paper used
Once too often to save money
I hope you remember this
My hand holding your
Much smaller hand
Walking down the street
Casting linked shadows before us as we go

My arms carrying you, sleep-heavy,
Up the stairs to your room
Where I placed a kiss on your forehead
And sang you a lullaby

My voice reading you a story,
Turning pages,
Leaning in to place kisses on the top of your head
While you explore new worlds

My hands tickling you
As you giggle and beg for more
And my head lying beside your head at night
My warmth keeping you warm as we drifted into sleep

When my eyesight has faded or my hearing has gone
When my body begins to return
To the stars from whence it comes
I hope that you will remember

That I have loved you with more than I am
With eternity
And constancy
My steadfast heart

Beating with joy and pride
Just for you
How I have loved you
Beyond time

Long before you were you
And long after I was me
I loved you before light
And after darkness

And all the times in between
And always will
When I am faded to gray and am less than I was
I'm still here-

Even when I'm gone-

I'll still be loving you.

A Letter to My Children

You didn't ask, but I'll tell you:
Everything.
That's what I want for you.
But mostly happiness
Joy brimming full and spilling over
Love, too, always love
The kind you have for everyone else
But also the kind you can wrap around yourself
Love that will keep you warm

Roots that extend into the earth
But wings that will help you fly
I know you can fly
I see it already, in your eyes
I'll nudge you out of the nest
Because that's what I do
But not for one second
Will you ever be unwelcome back in it
I will be a beacon
Calling you home
And you will always have a home here

But everything

That's my answer

I want everything in the world for you

But mostly love
And endless amounts of joy
And to know you can always
Always
Come home

(You are home to me.)

The Search for the Divine

I find you in the quiet spaces
Surrounded by the trees
Water lapping at the shore
In the buzzing of the bees
Idyllic surroundings
And peace inside my mind
I don't search in temples
Because I know what I would find

Ritual and flourish
A balm for souls, I know
But when I want to meet you
I know just where to go

I can climb a mountain
Or follow the nearest trail
I can sit inside a garden
Or a lake would do as well

But when the weather's raging
And keeps me from that space
I can reach inside me
And meet you in that place

In the quiet and the stillness
With a love so strong
No, I don't need a steeple
When you've been in me all along.

Prayer for the Non-Religious

we think prayer has form
crafted with careful salutation,
rote statement of gratitude,
tentative or heartfelt request,
and complimentary flourish of a finish.
we approach with humility or expectation
or something resembling faith or hope
or desperation.
we might add a postscript or two,
having forgotten something else
we're grateful for or needed
a last bid for attention.
our bodies fold up like envelopes,
hands clasped or not,
and we wet our lips
like licking a stamp
to send out our prayers.
we think prayer has anything at all to do with religion.
yet we've experienced prayer with no form at all.
a please uttered and repeated in anguish,
prayer reduced to a single word
sent out with little direction but so much intention,
the worship of bodies,
those murmured
or screamed
appeals to a deity
meant only to be shared between worshippers,

the bargaining of grief as we balk at loss,
push against it to keep it away,
offer trades and deals
if only we can keep what it is we want,
our gratitude —
because if that's not a prayer
I don't know what a prayer is,
our love —
the greatest act of faith.
we think we have to pair religion and prayer
as if one is broken without the other,
and yet kindness is a prayer,
an act of compassion sent out
and empathy is a prayer,
recognizing our shared humanity.
our breath is prayer,
the movement of our bodies,
the moment we fall in love,
the moment our hearts break,
birth and death,
our lives and whether we live them
or waste them. we pray.
to science, to nature, to love —
it seems we all pray to love
to last, to stay.
even if we're not religious,
we pray.

My Original Sin

the labyrinth path I follow
I'm not sure where it will end
it branches and twists inside me
around every new corner it bends
but I will still journey inward
I will follow the choices I've made
I will trace their roots even deeper
to see where the paths were once laid

I will search out the darkness
the one that sent me careening with fear
I will search out the needs I don't speak of
the ones that have held my hurts near

I will trace them back to their origin
I will find where they begin
I will spend time uncovering
my own and original sin

not born in me but learned
not made in me but decided
I will find the way back to my soul
I will follow the light that has guided

my steps as I walk this path
toward the truth that I require
the labyrinth leads, and I follow
this soul path that's taking me higher.

Frayed Sweater Souvenir

You give me your soft sweater
And say it's mine to keep
Then leave me in the morning
While I am still asleep

The edges are softly fraying
Unwinding at the seams
But I hold tight together
Used to many broken dreams

I take off your soft sweater
Leave it lying on the floor
Stripped down, cold, uncovered
But I won't need it anymore

I stretch out on the surface
Reclaiming every inch of space
I wonder if you'll even miss me
Or if you'll soon forget my face

Lovers come and leave again
Frayed sweater souvenir
You said you loved me in the night
And in the morning disappeared.

A Toast to What Once Was – And Is No Longer

My heart is beating inside my chest
I swear I once gave it all to you
Yet, find it beating as though it never left
A broken rhythm since we've been through

Your pain weighs heavier than mine ever will
And my love is stronger than you'll ever see clear
My heart on my sleeve leaks a bright red spill
Cut against the barbed wire you fashion of fear

My love is a thing you can neither see nor hear
A bright flashing light against the darkness of pain
I've spent years of my life wishing you near
Strawberry-stained lips still taste the shape of your name

I toast what we once were with a glass of champagne
The sweet clash against bitter — can you still taste it?
Then stretch into child's pose and connect with my breath
It seemed a better idea than just getting wasted

I once drank away sorrows and chased after pleasure
And held myself tightly through nightscapes of terror
I held every man up to your measure
Until I finally I met my own eyes in the mirror

Now I nourish with sweat instead of the fall of my tears
I'm healing this heart because I won't find another
One day, we'll love with more hope than fear
But we both know that we won't love each other.

Temptation

I run my fingers slowly
Over your skin
Light touch, a stroke, a moan—
And only then

Will my lips follow
To take their place
Slow and wet and hot
My tongue will trace

Your name and mine,
The holy fires light
To burn with candle flames
Into the night

The sun will rise,
But I cannot
let you sleep
Without tempting you,
again,
Into the deep.

Invulnerable: a 9 Act-Poem

Act I

I have held on
Far too long
To an illusion
The idea of epic love
You promised
With your eyes
I watched it
Dissolve there
Betrayal
Still feels like lies
But you never did see
Mine

The way I let you think
You knew me
The way I let you hold
My skin and melt my bones
All liquid heat
And beating heart
But I never let you
See my soul
Hoping if I only gave you
Pieces
When you left,
I'd still be
Whole.

Act II

It seems strange
That you doubt
The validity of grief
Until I remember
All the times
I wept alone
In my house on my own
Laughing with you
Between weeping
Into a muted phone

I silenced the line
Until I could speak
Without my voice breaking
Or shaking
Until it was easy
To make you believe
I was fine
A nightmare
With no end in waking
And no relief
With time

Still, you couldn't know
What I never let you see
What good would it do
To show you
When you stopped
Loving me
My tears were real

When you left
My voice on the line
Was even
And strong
Like you leaving me
Didn't feel like the world
Was wrong
And I didn't,
And would never,
Belong

But trusting you
Would have been
The end
Of me

It wouldn't have stopped
You leaving anyway
Wouldn't have made you
care
Enough to stay
Grief to me has
Always been for me alone
I've always cried
In bathrooms
In closets
Quiet places
Anywhere I could be
Alone

So, now I'm telling you
What you never knew
I muted the phone
When I was breaking down
Held it to my belly
While I screamed
Dropped, weeping,
To my knees
While I removed
Your pictures
From my walls

Cried heartfelt,
Wrenching tears
While stumbling
Down those halls

You only ever heard me
Be terribly strong
Isn't it funny
That was the illusion
All along.

Act III

I was a heart
Well-hidden
Aching to be known
A fortress
Of protections
Suffering alone

Your heart
Was a mystery
I could never solve
Like morning's mist
In sunlight
I watched you dissolve

We weren't oil and water
But a locked door
And an illusion
I was lost in love

You came to a different
Conclusion

I had a cracked
Open heart
You never wanted
To find
I nearly decided to
Trust you
When you started
Changing your mind

I was Alice
Always falling
You were a rabbit
On the run
Everyone is mad here
We're not the only ones.

Act IV

Time.
It's what everyone says
You have to use
To patch up a bleeding
heart
To make it
Almost-new

But Vincent told me once
Time does not bring relief
You all have lied
And I felt that truth
Dismissed the age-old
advice
As the ignorance
Of youth

Because time merely
Passes on its own
Broken hearts heal in
jagged lines
If you don't look
Too closely
You might believe
We're fine

Time is not the hero
We once thought
I am not as brave as I used
to be
Hope's a flickering flame
At best
I feel the wind blowing
Inside of me.

Act V

The only way time can heal
Is to forget
When memories begin
To fall away
But the strangest thing
I've experienced yet
Is to hope the memories
Of you will stay

I don't want the love erased
Even broken
I have loved your heart so
well
For time to take those
Cherished moments from
me
Is to plunge me
Straight into my hell

Because even though
No one's loved me well
I have loved with fervent
intent
I have lived my life
As if it is passing
Every second loving
Every moment spent

Time heals nothing
Hearts don't heal alone
Love just is, even when
lovers leave
We can pray for time
That pitiless god
To intervene
Or finally break and admit
To heal,
We have to grieve.

Act VI

Some of us
Don't learn how to lean
Never learned to accept
A helping hand
Trauma at the root
Wraps the whole tree
In ways looking in
You'll never understand

This isn't the life
I carefully planned
This is the one I built
From ash
Gently I wrap up my hand
In bandages
To heal from holding
carefully
The match

I was always better
On my own
Standing tall
A forest of one
Never stood inside
Another's shadow
Or close enough
To share
The storm or sun

And when I fall
Will anyone hear
The sound
How long will I wait
To even be found
Will they step over
The devastation
Walking carefully around

Some of us
Grow all on our own
We never lean
And never trust
And never learn
We don't have to be
Alone.

Act VII

I'll let you touch me
And get underneath my skin
But I won't let you
Truly know me
My heart's a place
You can't get in

I've been a rest stop
For broken, tired men
Made it easy for them
To stay a while
And then go again

Never letting them
Close enough to know me
Only ever letting them
Hold the old me
Not the one emerging
To shed this skin
That one will learn
To let a good one in.

Act VIII

Standing here reflected
I see my face
Clear of my artifice
Aware of my mistakes
I take off this worn armor
There's nothing left to lose
I am scarred, imperfect
And still worthy for you to choose
I am not invulnerable
I'm fragile, soft, and bruised

Act IX

For a while, I loved so fearlessly
I wish the one I'd loved wholly had been me
I know I'll never be fearless like that again
That's how I know
I'm ready to begin.

Lifelines: A Date with Time

Nature tattoos time
In fine lines across my face
Sends spiders skittering over my hands
To build the most delicate of webs
Threaded lifelines I cannot read, or plan
Passing days attempt to fade and weather
Yet, my spine is strong
My mind — still sharp and fast
My eyes can skewer or see
Straight through you
An oracle you keep looking past
Unknowing that the youth you claim is fleeting
And that an age so great is the only goal
To live well and live long is so precious
Before we turn to ash or fill a hole
I watch the lines grow with fear and wonder
And wish there was a hand
Holding my own
Still, I know that death is a jealous lover
There's no avoiding him getting you
Alone
But I've made a home of these fragile bones
I am loathe to leave this life behind
Without first giving away this heart to hold
To someone who could keep it safe
Through time —
And count themselves lucky to be mine —
Because the end is written in these lines.

He

He took my breath
Took my time
Took my heart
Left this rhyme

He took my hand
Took my mouth
Took my belief
And left this doubt

He turned my words
Into a thunderous roar
Into a wail of grief
Then closed the door

He didn't want me anymore

Then HE took my breath
And took my hand
And earned my trust
Because he understands

That I need my words
Need love returned
And have given too easy
What was unearned

He held my heart
And met my mouth
Gave me reason to believe
To discard the doubt

He doesn’t take your place
He’s made his own
These days, I don’t stand
In love alone

But stand by him
Our hands entwined
From grief, emerged
The stars aligned

You left my heart
He holds it close
You needed to consider
He already knows.

Interior: A Storm Warning

Candles send shadows dancing along the walls
A slow undulation keeping time
The needle scratch against the record spinning
Accompanies the sound of pouring wine

Tree branch trails fingers along the glass
A tap, tap, tap as if in time
To ask to cut into the dance, but this dance card's full

I run a finger down a spine
Pages fall open as welcome as a lover
The needle lifts, then quiet, now a turning
Before the needle drops a single kiss
To send another love song slowly spinning

I turn a page and take another sip
Words from the past pour into the room
Where candle shadows against walls are waltzing

Tree branches tap in time
To notes held and rustled paper
Candles burn
A pause, a break, a sip
A turning page
Slow wax melt, a ballerina turn
A voice from the other side lives again

Turns shadow partners and pages
Trees tap but can't cut in
Set the needle back
And play my song
Again.

Exterior: Thunderstorm Warning

The wind began its long campaign
A simmered sound turning to screams
When persuasiveness doesn't do the trick
It tries to rip the leaves from the trees
Rumbles send children scrambling from their dreams
To cozy into Mother's bed
Where they can lay in safety sleeping
Sweet dreams chase nightmares from their heads
But outside all is cold and frenzy
Branches whipping, protect and defend
Tapping windows, testing entry
But no one inside will relent
Instead shutters close and curtains draw
Houses dark and secrets kept
Locking out the wind, a street corner preacher
Who spit-screams to strangers to repent
While inside Mother murmurs and rolls
Against her sleeping child,
Curled together warm and safe
While outside in the weeping wild
Of tantrum winds calling howls
And scratching branches whipping round
Until at last the wind slowly settles
The calm of darkness dropping down
Tree frogs hop on the garden wall
Crickets strike up the band again
Branches rest and seem to sigh
Flowers soak the raindrops in
Mother sighs and children dream
And tree branches finally drift to sway
Now lulled by a gentle wind
Leaves dance across the empty sidewalk
No one awake to applaud their spin.

Performance Art

Curl into a comma
To shield the heart
Wings beating fast
Against a cage
The lash of angry words
Strikes down
I leave my body
On the stage
And sit in the darkness
Now to observe
The curtain hides
The trembling of birds
No audience applauds
No one can see
The mask you reveal
Only to me.

The Stars Will Keep My Secrets

The hush of nighttime is a balm
When I step outside in the cool night air
My feet are bare, the world is calm
The stars above don't seem to care
About my life down on this earth
My troubled loves or hard-fought wins
Yet they've endured from my birth
And will shine on when my journey ends

I find comfort in their distant light
I find solace on this quiet street
In this moment, the world seems right
My puppy sniffles around my feet
And pulls the leash toward the door
A reminder that I still need my rest

I look above until I can look no more
And lock the stars inside my chest
Where they will light my way to sleep
And all my secrets they will keep.

Hold Me in the Nighttime

I hold myself as I fall asleep
These arms have never let me down
Have never dropped me
From the heights of love
These arms have always kept me
Safe and sound

I whisper words of love
To me alone
Because I've survived life on my own
Without a hand holding mine
With gritted teeth and ramrod spine
My love for me has been
My only home

I walk myself through this world
And I am not afraid
Even though I'd like a hand in mine
Even though I wish you'd stayed
But I can love this
Life I've made.

A Self-Love Potion

Gather vials of stoppered glass
Line them up in a careful row
Pull back the heavy curtains
To catch the moon's soft glow
Fill three with water and three with oil
Fill another with soil or sand
Leave one empty to stand alone
Label each with a steady hand

The first three bottles are to drink
The next three are for taking care
The other one is for grounding you
The last one has space to spare
Then leave them to absorb the moon
And then a day in sunlight, too
Then as the sun sets on the day
There's more work we must do

To the first six bottles, we place a drop
Of lemon, mint, or herb
Into the soil, we place a key
But the last one's not disturbed
And into the first six, we place our hopes,
Our wishes, and our dreams
In the seventh, we focus our work
And the last is not what it seems

The first three nights, we sip from one
Of each of the first three stoppered vials
While focusing on what we want
Then we meditate a while

The next three nights, we turn to oil
Massaging hope into our skin

We focus on the life we need
We open ourselves and let it in
The seventh night, we take the vial
And remove the hidden key
For four more nights, we keep it close
To let the grounding be

Then on the 12th night and the last
The empty vial stands alone
Beside it now, we place the key
To our hearts and homes
We focus on it, see it clear
Our whole lives until this time
There is no incantation here
No studied words or rhyme

There is only abundant love
Flowing in a steady motion
We draw to us all the love
That we've put into this potion
And no Prince Charming will ride his steed
To champion our cases
We've not wished for the strength of ten
Or for pretty faces

And we've not drawn to us a person
Who would not be beguiled
We've not tampered with what is
Or the purest love defiled
Instead we've focused on our hearts
We've cleared out our minds
We've meditated on the love
Our hearts still hope to find

And there's no danger to this spell
No more power in this rite
Than what we create from our self-love
And what we bring in light

Put the vials of stoppered glass
Upon the shelf and go
There is so much love in this world
Than you or I can know.

Acknowledgements

This book is for the women in my life who have supported my journey. The last few years have had some incredible challenges, not the least of which was a badly broken heart and a struggle that ended in a PMDD diagnosis. I could not have healed without the help of Coleen, my therapist, and the many friends and professionals who help me manage my pain and the ups and downs of this disorder.

As always, my deepest gratitude and love go out to my children. I also want to take a moment to honor the memory of both Mary Lou Beasley and Margie Sanders Peoples, my grandmothers. The circle is open but never broken. Thank you for everything.

Other Titles by Crystal Jackson

The Heart of Madison Series

Left on Main
Right on Walton
Deep in the Heart of Madison
Waiting for the Girl Next Door

Poetry Books

My Words are Whiskey
Letters to Lost Lovers
A Solitary Witch Brews Self-Love

About the Author

Crystal Jackson is a former therapist turned author. She is the author of the *Heart of Madison* series, *My Words Are Whiskey*, and *Letters to Lost Lovers*. Her work has been featured on Medium, News Break, Elite Daily, Your Tango, and The Good Men Project. When she's not writing for Medium and working on her next book, you can find Crystal traveling, paddle boarding, cycling, throwing axes badly but with terrifying enthusiasm, hiking, doing yoga, or curled up with her nose in a book in Madison, Georgia where she lives with one Welsh Terrier and two wild and wonderful children.

This is her third collaboration with Christina Nicole.

Follow her work at:

www.crystaljacksonwriter.com
www.facebook.com/CrystalJackson.Writer
www.instagram.com/CrystalJackson.Writer
twitter.com/@cjacksonwriter
www.medium.com/@CrystalJackson

About the Artist

Christina Nicole is a self-taught artist and freelance writer. She thrives on expressing herself through various medium and styles ranging from minimalist illustration to realism. Her work primarily focuses on themes such as social issues, women's issues, and the overall human condition. Her desire is to cultivate a sense of connection with our universal experiences through art and the written word. When she's not pouring her heart out onto paper she can be found reading as many indie books as she can get her hands on and spending time with her husband and three little humans in their little house in the south.

This is her third collaboration with Crystal Jackson.

Stalk her work here:

www.facebook.com/Christinanicoleart
www.instagram.com/christina.nicole_
www.medium.com/@_christinanicole
Twitter.com/@_ladyhorror
www.instagram.com/ladyhorrorart/

www.ingramcontent.com/pod-product-compliance
Lightning Source LLC
LaVergne TN
LVHW050319160826
845677LV00014B/3470

* 9 7 9 8 3 5 3 0 3 3 6 5 3 *